Confucianism
CHINA

Rob Waring, *Series Editor*

HEINLE
CENGAGE Learning™

Australia • Brazil • Japan • Korea • Mexico • Singapore • Spain • United Kingdom • United States

Words to Know

This story is about the country of China, its history, the beliefs of some of its people, and its future.

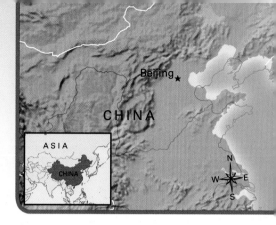

 China's History. Read the sentences. Then complete the paragraph with the correct form of the underlined words or phrases.

A <u>dynasty</u> is a ruling family that holds power in a country's government.
<u>Harmony</u> is peaceful cooperation.
<u>In decline</u> means getting worse or failing.
<u>Philosophy</u> is a special system of knowledge developed by a great thinker.
A <u>warlord</u> is a leader of a fighting group.

In ancient times, China was governed by a series of ruling families, including the Zhou [dʒoʊ] (1)_____. The Zhou ruled from 1046-256 B.C., but at around 500 B.C., the dynasty was (2)_____ and things were slowly falling apart. Local (3)_____ were constantly fighting. It was around this time that a great thinker named Confucius traveled China and tried to teach that peace and (4)_____ were most important for a healthy society. However, it was not until the Han dynasty came to power in 206 B.C. that his (5)_____ was finally put into practice.

B **Confucius.** Read the paragraph. Then complete each definition with the correct word.

Confucius (551–479 B.C.) was a great Chinese thinker, historical figure, and philosopher. His teachings formed the foundation for a great deal of the Chinese way of thinking. Confucius thought individuals should have good morals and always do the right thing. He also felt that people should have strong ethics and behave in a respectful manner. Confucianism is considered to have been a great influence on Eastern thought, and can be compared to the influence of the Greek philosopher Socrates on the West.

1. E_____ are related to correct behavior.
2. M_____ are related to judging what is right or wrong.
3. The f_____ is the idea upon which something is based.
4. C_____ is the way of thinking based on the Chinese thinker, Confucius.
5. A p_____ is a great thinker who studies the general truths and beliefs about humankind, the world, and life.

Confucius lived from 551–479 B.C.

3

China is one of the largest and oldest countries in the world. Millions of Chinese people share a rich history that has lasted for thousands of years. Over these thousands of years, China has been influenced by numerous great leaders and thinkers. One of its greatest and most famous philosophers was Confucius, who lived from 551 to 479 B.C.

Confucius is a well-known figure throughout the entire world. His way of thinking has influenced not only China, but many Asian countries. This story is about the impact of Confucius on modern China, but to fully understand his influence, we first must examine the past.

🎧 CD 1, Track 05

In ancient times, China was ruled by a series of dynasties. Around 500 B.C., the Zhou dynasty governed central China; however, its rulers were weak and the dynasty was in decline. Local warlords fought among themselves for land and power, and family members often fought one another over property and money. The country of China was caught up in a dark period of war and unhappiness. There was a lack of **justice**[1] in the country, and ordinary people were suffering. It was at this time in history that Confucius lived and taught.

Confucius' way of teaching people was to travel across China and talk to them. He hoped to **convince**[2] the people that his moral and ethical ideas about society could restore order, justice, and **prosperity**[3] to China. His ideas have come to be known as Confucianism, and are the foundation for an entire philosophical belief system.

---

[1] **justice:** the law when it is applied or carried out in a fair way
[2] **convince:** cause someone to believe that something is worth doing or true
[3] **prosperity:** a good economic period

One of Confucius's central beliefs was that a healthy society was dependent upon peace and harmony. He believed that these societal characteristics depended on having the correct and proper conduct in key relationships between people. Two examples of these key relationships are the one between a parent and child and the one between ruler and subject. Confucius thought that if these relationships were not properly conducted, there would be disorder in society.

Unfortunately, the leaders of the time were warlords. They did not govern their lands by forming positive relationships with their subjects as Confucius taught. As a result of this and other issues, the Zhou dynasty continued to decline and the situation for ordinary Chinese people got worse and worse.

Eventually, Confucius **retired**[4] and focused on teaching his disciples, or followers. After his death, his disciples developed and **expanded upon**[5] his ideas through the centuries. Slowly over the years, the philosophy of Confucius grew significantly in importance. Finally, 300 years after Confucius died, the Han dynasty **adopted**[6] his philosophy as its official government policy. Centuries after Confucius's death, his ideas had at last become an essential part of the Chinese way of life.

Confucianism became an important part not only of the Han dynasty, but of other dynasties as well. His ideas are still a significant influence on various aspects of Chinese culture today. He is often referred to as 'The Master' and for some, his words have become a code of conduct by which to live.

---

[4]**retire:** stop working
[5]**expand upon:** grow larger; make greater and more detailed
[6]**adopt:** come to accept as one's own

The Confucian Academy and Museum in Chaozhou, China

Sequence the Events

What is the correct order of the events? Write numbers.

_____ Confucius stopped teaching.

_____ Confucius traveled across China.

_____ The Han rulers adopted Confucianism.

_____ The followers of Confucius developed his beliefs.

One of these codes of conduct is an extremely important example of the impact of Confucianism on modern Chinese family relationships. Confucius, or The Master, said, "A youth should be respectful of his elders." The respect that young people show toward their parents, grandparents, and other older people, is still an important aspect of Chinese family life today. Several generations of family members often live and work together, and most children are expected to follow their parents' wishes and do what is best for the family. The needs of the family almost always come before the desires of individuals. Traditionally, sons carry on the family name and support their parents when they are older and require care.

What about education? How can we see the influence of Confucianism in such an important area of life? On this, The Master once questioned, "Is it not pleasant to learn with a constant **perseverance**[7] and **application**?"[8] Confucius felt that learning should be a pleasant experience and one that should be approached with joy.

Nowadays, learning and education are still extremely important to the people of China. From a very early age, students learn to study hard and to respect their teachers. Throughout the history of China and many other cultures, an education has been the primary way that people could move beyond their social class. It's often considered an opportunity to move up in the world and attain success in a number of ways.

---

[7]**perseverance:** continued and determined effort to achieve a goal
[8]**application:** determined work over a period of time

More than five million young people in China graduate from College every year. When these Chinese students leave college, many of them seek jobs in China. Others choose to explore their options by going abroad. In fact, Chinese graduates have traveled around the entire world looking for new opportunities and new possibilities. Over 30 million Chinese people now live in other parts of the world, including Southeast Asia, the United States, Canada, and other countries and regions.

The influence of Confucius also spread to the area of money and wealth. He is quoted as saying: "**Virtue**[9] is the **root**;[10] wealth is the result." In other words, Confucius appeared to feel that if people were good and hardworking, they would become rich. Today, many Chinese people continue to believe in hard work to build lives for themselves and their families. This reflects a **fundamental**[11] principle of Confucianism: those who are dutiful and live in harmony with others will always prosper.

---

[9]**virtue:** the quality of goodness in a person
[10]**root:** the origin or cause of something
[11]**fundamental:** basic; very important

Because Confucianism is often associated with China's past, many people are not fully aware of the considerable influence it still has on present-day Chinese society. Confucianism is a philosophy that is 2,500 years old, and it has been at the center of Chinese civilization and culture for centuries. Such an ancient philosophy does not simply disappear or lose its influence; some still consider it to be at the very core of modern Chinese society.

And what of the future? Based on the history of the last centuries, it is likely that Confucianism will continue to influence Chinese society for many years to come. As China and the world continue to change, this country's future will surely be impacted by its past.

Summarize

Imagine you are telling someone about the influence of Confucius's ideas on modern China. Write or speak about one of the following topics:

- family

- education

- work

After You Read

1. In paragraph 2 on page 4, the word 'examine' is closest in meaning to:
   A. investigate
   B. criticize
   C. memorize
   D. engineer

2. In 500 B.C., Chinese people fought about each of the following EXCEPT:
   A. land
   B. money
   C. suffering
   D. power

3. Why does the writer explain the lack of order and justice in ancient China?
   A. to give details about why no one wanted to listen to Confucius
   B. to describe the situation in China that Confucius hoped to change
   C. to point out the impact Confucius had in Chinese society
   D. to teach about the beginning of the Zhou dynasty

4. The relationship between a _____ and a _____ is an example of a key relationship.
   A. friend, enemy
   B. sister, brother
   C. boy, girl
   D. mother, daughter

5. Who was most responsible for spreading Confucianism to the people of China?
   A. the Zhou dynasty
   B. Chinese philosophers
   C. Confucius' followers
   D. the warlords

6. An appropriate heading for paragraph 2 on page 10 is:
   A. The Master's Ideas Rejected
   B. An Influential Philosophy
   C. Han Dynasty Fights Confucius
   D. Country Makes Confucius Ruler

7. On page 13, 'they' refers to:
   A. parents
   B. sons
   C. grandparents
   D. individuals

8. The writer suggests Chinese children are:
   A. disobedient
   B. selfish
   C. wasteful
   D. respectful

9. What's the purpose of paragraph 2 on page 14?
   A. to discuss the difficult job of Chinese teachers
   B. to explain the significance of education in China
   C. to give an example of Confucianism
   D. to describe one typical Chinese student

10. According to Confucius, which is a result of hard work?
   A. respect
   B. prosperity
   C. trouble
   D. belief

11. In paragraph 1 on page 18, the term 'associated' can be replaced by:
   A. separated
   B. activated
   C. connected
   D. carried

12. A suitable heading for page 18 is:
   A. Ancient Thinking Shapes Modern Life
   B. Confucianism Discovered in China
   C. Future China Impacts Past China
   D. World Moves Away from Confucianism

Favorite
CONFUCIUS
Sayings

POSTED: *Carlos on Friday, Aug. 30 @ 7:12 pm*

Confucius had a lot to say about how to live a good life. What's your favorite Confucius saying? Leave a comment about your favorite saying and tell us why you like it. In the survey in the side menu, you can vote for your favorite!

"I hear and I forget. I see and I remember. I do and I understand."
POSTED: *Rebecca on Wednesday, Sept. 4 @ 8:20 am:*

My favorite saying is, *"I hear and I forget. I see and I remember. I do and I understand."* It's not clear whether Confucius said this or one of his followers, but I agree completely with the statement. For example, I'm learning German and it takes hard work to learn new vocabulary words. Hearing them and reading them is a good start, but using them in my own speech and writing is what really helps me to learn.

"What you do not wish done to yourself, do not do to others."
POSTED: *Tam on Tuesday, Sept. 3 @ 7:00 pm:*

I like *"What you do not wish done to yourself, do not do to others."* best. Confucius wasn't the only one to promote this idea. Most religions agree with this concept. To me, it's the most important life rule: treat others as you would like to be treated. Just the other day, I was with a friend in class and she started talking badly about a classmate of ours. I kept on thinking about how bad our classmate would feel if he knew she was saying such terrible things! I know I wouldn't like it!

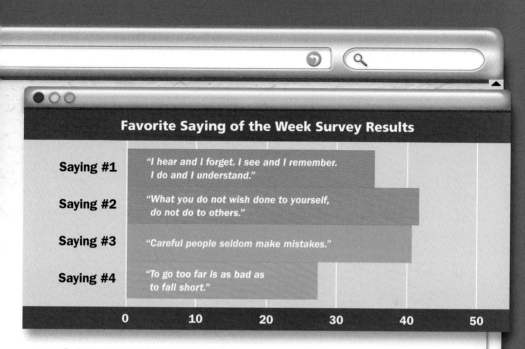

Favorite Saying of the Week Survey Results

Saying #1	*"I hear and I forget. I see and I remember. I do and I understand."*
Saying #2	*"What you do not wish done to yourself, do not do to others."*
Saying #3	*"Careful people seldom make mistakes."*
Saying #4	*"To go too far is as bad as to fall short."*

0   10   20   30   40   50

"Careful people seldom make mistakes."
POSTED: Rosa on Sunday, Sept. 1 @ 2:00 pm:

"Careful people seldom make mistakes." is one of my favorites. I like to remind myself of this saying when taking a test or writing a paper in school. It's better to work slowly and pay close attention to details in order to avoid making unnecessary and sometimes costly mistakes. Taking your time and making an extra effort can often guarantee success.

"To go too far is as bad as to fall short."
POSTED: Andre on Saturday, Aug. 31 @ 2:15 pm:

My favorite is: *"To go too far is as bad as to fall short."* It means that to do too much of something is equally as bad as not doing enough. It's possible to not try hard enough and it is also possible to try too hard. For example, I wanted to lose a few kilos for a big party so I didn't eat enough and exercised all the time. In the end, I got really sick and tired from eating poorly and couldn't even go to the party! For me, it's important to find a balance between two extremes in order to achieve my goals.

CD 1, Track 06

Word Count: 370
Time: _____

Vocabulary List

adopt (10)
application (14)
Confucianism (3, 7, 10, 11, 13, 14, 17, 18)
convince (7)
dynasty (2, 7, 8, 10)
ethic (3, 7)
expand upon (10)
foundation (3, 7)
fundamental (17)
harmony (2, 8, 17)
in decline (2, 7, 8)
justice (7)
moral (3, 7)
perseverance (14)
philosopher (3, 4)
philosophy (2, 7, 10, 18)
prosperity (7)
retire (10)
root (17)
virtue (17)
warlord (2, 7, 8)